MIDDLE AGE RAGE

...and Other Male Indignities

Fred Shoenberg

Illustrations by Rob Edwards

SIMON AND SCHUSTER   NEW YORK

Designed by Susan Brooker/Levavi & Levavi
Manufactured in the United States of America
1   3   5   7   9   10   8   6   4   2
Library of Congress Cataloging-in-Publication Data

Shoenberg, Fred.
Middle age rage—and other male indignities.

1. Middle aged men—Psychology—Anecdotes,
facetiae, satires, etc.   2. Aging—Anecdotes,
facetiae, satires, etc.   I. Title.
BF724.6.S55   1987   155.6   86-31362
ISBN 0-671-60562-3

To my wife, Ina, who walked fearlessly with me, hand in hand into middle age, for her inspiration for this book and this life.

To my mother, who told me at the appropriate time in her life that she was too busy to be middle-aged. To my daughter, Amy, and son, Maco, who readily and unfailingly helped identify certain manifestations of a condition I had chosen to ignore.

To Michael Korda, who understood all perfectly from the beginning of this endeavor, even though he has managed to avoid middle age himself. And to my partner, Bill Hieber, whose silent indulgence of my absences, musings and sufferings was wonderfully eloquent.

You're the man for this book if:

     A) You understand the title.
     B) You need glasses to read it.
     C) You are only buying it for an older friend.

CONTENTS

Groan Up 11

Chapter 1
HOW TO TELL IF YOU ARE MIDDLE-AGED 17

Chapter 2
CORPUS DERELICTI 25

Chapter 3
EXERCISE AND THE MIDDLE-AGED MAN 47

Chapter 4
MIDDLE AGE SEX 59

Chapter 5
THE MIDDLE AGE PSYCHE 73

Chapter 6
HEALTH 85

Chapter 7
LIFE-STYLES OF THE MIDDLE-AGED MAN 93

Chapter 8
FUTURE SCHLOCK 107

Chapter 9
TRAVAIL BUREAU 115

Chapter 10
NOW THAT WE'RE HERE 119

Last Chapter
HOW TO AVOID MIDDLE AGE 127

GROAN UP

One morning last spring I got out of bed and my back didn't work. It wasn't serious—a pinched nerve or a muscle spasm—but you know how it is when you're busy with meetings, lunch dates, theater tickets to get. . . . There's no time to be crippled, so I was understandably upset.

Trying to put things right, I hobbled over to the telephone book to look up the number of a chiropractor I knew. While vainly searching for his name, I realized that for the past six or seven months I no longer had been able to read anything smaller than the *New York Post* headlines. Even worse, the reason I was helplessly straining my eyes to find the number was that I couldn't *remember* it, a problem that had been occurring with greater frequency every month.

I somehow got downstairs and crawled into a taxi, where all the way to my office the driver was saying something about someone of my age hanging upside down for twenty minutes every day—great for the spine, with only the minor risk of stroke.

Once in my office, I shuffled, hunched, toward my desk, dragging one foot. My colleagues, heartless game-players all, snickered: "Quasimodo—right? Big Foot?"

"Shut up, you insensitive fools," I shouted, trying not to appear hysterical. "There's something wrong with my back. Life is not a parlor game!"

Then, in an attempt to make me feel better, one of them came over and said, "At our age we have to expect things like this every once in a while. It's middle age, you know."

I didn't know and I didn't *want* to know! His life was spared only because he didn't wink at me, or poke his elbow in my ribs.

But there was no mistaking it. And I was furious. It seemed as if the day was the culmination of a series of minor irritations, breakdowns and indignities that, like the plagues, were mounting relentlessly. I expected pestilence and frogs.

Later that same day, a 35-year old businessman called me "sir." For some reason, that took me over the top. I felt a strange sort of flush. Then the rage—no longer suppressed—burst out in the open, uncontrolled.

Things *were* happening to me. *Was* this middle age? If so, how the hell did *I* get there?

Middle age, I thought, must be the accumulation of a lot of small short circuits and stress fractures, to the point where things begin to blink or break and you are at last forced to notice them.

Such was my introduction to the notion of middle age—the day I recognized my rage. My back is now okay, and I've bought a pair of glasses (I held out for another six months, though). Now I'm working on my head. But as you will see, my rage is totally justified, maybe even therapeutic. If you don't share it, you simply haven't reached middle age yet.

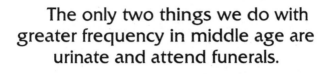

The only two things we do with greater frequency in middle age are urinate and attend funerals.

CHAPTER 1

HOW TO TELL IF YOU ARE MIDDLE-AGED

In the beginning . . .

*M*iddle age starts the morning you get up, go to the bathroom, look in the mirror and admit that you arc who you are going to be. Frightening moment. No more hero, composer, author, athlete or superman. This is it. You are who you are. No more dreams of glory, and no miracles. Just middle age!

The first challenge is to prevent this moment of truth. Let us keep doubt, paranoia and realism from seeping through the wall of faith, fantasy and adolescent behavior that has kept us moving and laughing all these years. We must shake off the notion that we are as old as the rest of the world says we are.

Most people cannot describe middle age to their own satisfaction—they know it's waiting out there, or they know they're in it. For some it starts at 30, for

some at 50 and for some it is always ahead but never reached. "Middle age" describes a state that does not have a chronology but rather a set of preconditions. One of the reasons we react strongly to it is because it defines a person who has a set of symptoms for which there is no disease.

Is there a cure?

Here's the bad news: There's no cure. No one is even *working* on one. The only way to avoid middle age is to become prematurely old.

Signs that You May Be Among Us

Not minding if someone else drives.

Deciding you want a younger doctor.

Producing a heretofore unheard sound when bending or kneeling.

Standing in a room for several moments trying to figure out why you went in there.

Calling one of your children by the dog's name.

Saying something for the first time that your father used to say and that you never liked.

Remembering your anniversary.

Shaving four feet from the mirror.

You could be a candidate for middle age if you can remember

Decoder Rings

Crinolines

Kaiser-Frasers

Mumblety-Peg

Johnny Ray

Fred Allen

Tom Mix

Tojo

Virgins

Wildroot Cream Oil

BB

Lucky Strike Green

Phrases to Avoid

Don't you know who I was?

That was my niece.

Before the war . . .

What was I saying?

I'll wait for the elevator.

What the hell do you mean, I'm less patient?

VISUAL DEPICTION OF LIFE AS AN ALP

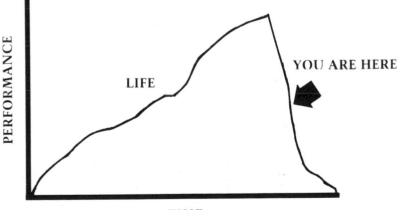

Recognizing Middle Age Rage in Others

*T*he man who has trained his grandchildren to call him by his first name.

The man who feels he must assert himself everywhere under any circumstance, like cursing loudly at an automatic toll machine.

The older man with a fast sports car so small and inaccessible that only Herve Villechaize would be comfortable driving it.

The man swayed by flattery from almost any source.

The man who, no matter how tight the lid, how heavy the load or how stuck the window, says: "Here, let me do that" in the presence of a younger man, usually his son. (Result: paralysis within 12 hours.)

The man who thinks he has something sage to say—and worse, that someone is interested in hearing it.

I stopped a middle-aged person in the street and asked, "Do you think mid-life crisis is a consequence of ignorance or apathy?" His answer: "I don't know and I don't care."

Middle age is that span in life when you admit to no longer being young and deny being old.

CHAPTER 2

CORPUS DERELICTI

Middle-Aged Body Owner's Manual

(Covering model years 1920 through 1945)

For use when each of us realizes he is driving around in a lemon.

General Information

This booklet covers bodies with standard equipment well past the "break-in period."

Important: At age 39 all warranties run out. Do *not* apply for free part replacements.

If you have problems not covered by this manual or correctable by your local serviceman, appeal directly to the maker.

Trouble Shooting

Areas of most common complaints:
Starting difficulties
Poor performance
Exhaust problems
Misfiring
Loss of power
Chassis deterioration

Periodic Maintenance and Tune-up

Recommended every six months: See your local mechanic.

Check fluid and pressure levels.

Caution: Do not try to turn back the odometer. True mileage can be determined by examining other parts of the body.

Surface changes will occur and squeaks and cracks in the chassis should also be expected. These are normal.

Fuel Systems

Use unsalted fuel only.

Older type fuels (no matter how well they once worked) will destroy machinery.

Fuels should not be taken in late at night, and never again up to the "full" level.

Rear Suspension

At this point you are going to have to live with it as is. As bad as it may look, it is not dangerous.

Gears

Do not be alarmed: There is no reverse.

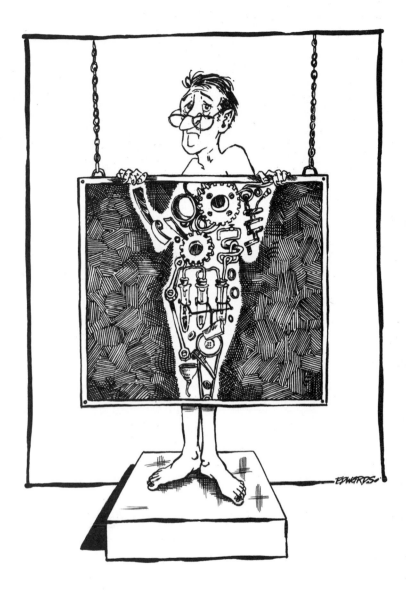

General Warnings

Equipment should be started slowly in the morning and not run at full power after dark. *Never jump start.*

> Middle-aged man is the only
> endangered species not headed for
> extinction.

Optical Allusions

*L*ate one night I was sitting in the den watching TV. The door to the kitchen was open and when I got up to go to bed, I noticed a roach poised on the white counter near the sink. Slowly, quietly, I removed a shoe and inched my way into the kitchen through the shaft of blue-gray TV light. Bam! Got it.

I turned on the light, lifted my shoe, and found that I had killed a raisin!

Focal Points

I was recently at a big meeting on Wall Street for a new underwriting and found myself standing next to a former business associate. As we chatted, we were each handed a prospectus of the company under discussion. As I lifted the prospectus to read it, I made a slight adjustment in the distance between my eyes and the document.

"Aha," said my friend, "you're at that stage. Here, try these." He handed me his pair of reading glasses.

I tried to read with them; no good. "Too strong," I said.

"That's because these are number twenty-eights. You need number twenty-sixes. That's what we all start with."

"What in the world are you talking about?"

"Go to New Jersey—it's against the law in New York—find a big Woolworth's. Go to the eyeglass counter and buy, for under ten dollars, a pair of number twenty-sixes. They come in tortoise shell and black. You'll save a fortune—probably two hundred dollars between the doctors and the glasses. And you'll be very happy."

"I have no time to schlepp to New Jersey in search of pieces of magnifying glass snapped into cheap frames which I probably don't need anyway."

"Wait," my friend pressed on. "I still have my twenty-sixes at home and I can't use them anymore. Meet me at the Exchange for lunch tomorrow and I'll bring them for you."

"Great! Thanks. Tomorrow."

Next day at lunch, as promised, he appeared with the glasses. We sat down and I picked up the menu and put on the glasses.

"Son of a bitch," said I. "They're perfect." I was furious.

I am still furious. Now I can see, but mostly red.

At middle age a picture is worth
only eight hundred words.

After the Fall

*H*air, although of little use, appears to have great value. We all seem to want it.

In middle age, however, most of us are receding, thinning or balding. And we respond by shaping, dyeing, spraying, curling, straightening, weaving, transplanting, implanting and buying hair—befitting acts of mid-life lunacy. But some things are at once outré and declassé:

1.

Allowing a tuft of hair behind one ear to grow to a length of several feet and then whipping it around on top of your head.

2.

Tinting your hair so that in certain lights you look prematurely purple, or dyeing it black except for a flash of white at each temple.

3.

Combing your remaining hair forward on all parts of your head as if you've been spending your life with a stiff wind at your back.

4.

Wearing a toupee of a different color from your own hair if your own hair can also be seen.

*T*here are always options, of course. You can live with what you've got, or if you absolutely cannot deal with bald, you can convert to Orthodox Judaism and wear a hat all the time. I have opted for the first.

For a while, it seemed a miracle was at hand; a new drug, minoxidil, reputedly grew hair on approximately 30 percent of heads tested. Minoxidil is made from, among other things, ground-up high blood pressure pills (and very small cameras?), and it seems ready for FDA approval. Since the solution is applied to the scalp manually, it is conceivable that those using it will also have the world's hairiest hands.

My wife and I recently attended the wedding of some friends in Florida. It was a wonderfully thought-out ceremony that included a professional photographer videotaping the guests all evening. A month or so later we got a chance to view the edited tapes. At one point the camera (with very bright lights attached) picked up the back of a tall man with a bald spot on his head talking to several other people. Someone in the room viewing the tapes with us said, "Oh, look, there's Fred."

"That's not me," I said. "That guy is bald in back." There ensued a hushed silence during which everyone stared at me incredulously. "Oh, come on," I said, "you're all gaslighting me." I was quickly ushered into the bathroom and placed between the medicine cabinet and a hand mirror to view the ugly and naked truth.

I handled it. I know how to deal with that sort of shock. I can take it. No problem. I can deal with this. No sweat.

It's hair, after all, not blood.

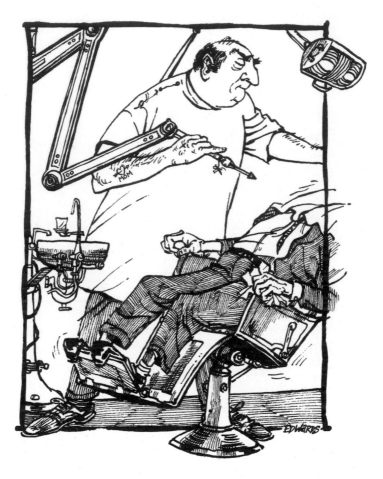

... And Then There Were None

When you get old enough and have enough money, you develop something called periodontal disease. It has to do with plaque—a substance on teeth in which bacteria frolic, eating away at your gums and bone. Soon you have severe bone loss, your teeth begin to wobble, fall out of your mouth, and otherwise behave badly. Even if you do go through periodontal surgery, there is no assurance that your teeth still won't fall out anyway.

I am going through it now.

Does it hurt? Well, yes, but how do you measure pain? A friend from Texas came to New York to have his hemorrhoids removed (or whatever they do to them). During his convalescence, I asked him if the pain after the operation was as bad as I had heard. He said, "Let me put it this way. The first time I went to the can after surgery, I ripped the towel rack out of the wall." After periodontal work I understood that.

> Middle age is nature's way of
> showing a sense of humor.

If Looks Could Kill

After thirty-five years of marriage Sam's wife died. At the end of a proper mourning period, Sam looked at himself and said, "Life is not over. I can go out and have some fun and perhaps meet a nice, younger woman and—who knows what?" Over an eighteen-month period Sam joined a gym to tone up, lost forty pounds, bought a toupee, had all his teeth capped, got a nose job, had a little tuck taken in his chin, grew a mustache, got contact lenses and bought a new youth-oriented wardrobe with elevator shoes. Finally one day he was ready to step out—he loved what he saw in the mirror. Unfortunately, that night Sam died and went to heaven, whereupon he met God. "God," said Sam, "I was a kind and loving husband, a wonderful father and grandfather, a charitable person, and honest and hardworking in my business. I was just about to start a new life. Why did you do this?" "Sam," replied God, "to tell you the truth, I didn't recognize you."

Process of Elimination

*T*hirty years ago in Paris I would go to the john with yesterday's newspaper because the chances were that there would be no paper in the W.C. Today, modern middle-aged man is incapable of voiding himself without the use of literature, and I don't mean yesterday's newspaper.

This often has a Pavlovian effect. For twenty-five years I have been reading *The Wall Street Journal* in the bathroom early in the morning. Now when someone shows me a *Wall Street Journal* to point something out later in the day or on a weekend, I get a strange sensation in my bowels.

Nouvelle Queasiness

You wake up at 4:15 A.M., having intercepted signals from your bladder to your brain. Your bladder is awaiting instructions. Your brain is holding up for a minute to give you a chance to decide where you would like to be when the return signal is sent. You allow your eyes to open a crack to survey your immediate surroundings. Nothing looks familiar. Oh, God. Concentrate a moment. Now you've got it. You're in a hotel room. What city? What's the difference what city? The signal is getting louder. You don't want to get up in a strange room if you don't know what city you're in. Are you crazy? This is getting painful. It's either San Francisco or L.A. Great, get up; we're talking urgent now.

You struggle into a sitting position; discomfort increases. You're on your feet now and making slowly for the dark opening in the wall. The impact tells you it's a mirror—dope. Try again, and this time the cold tiles under your feel tell you you're in the right place. Don't turn the light on; it'll just wake you up. What do you mean, don't turn the light on? Are you expecting divine intervention? Radar? Don't argue—can't hold out any longer—we're in the red zone. Here we go. You pick up the seat just as the brain hits the release button and that warm familiar feeling overcomes you as pain subsides. Standing there in a strange room, in a strange city, in the dark, barefoot on a cold floor with your eyes closed, you sense something is missing. No alarm, just the feeling that some component is absent. Smiling warmly with the happy thought of going back to bed you reach for the flushing mechanism and instantly realize what is missing. There is no handle. There is no sound of water. You can't flush a hamper.

While we're on the subject, you don't do even that so well anymore. There seems to be a lack of power. You don't get started like you mean business and, worse, you can't seem to actually finish. Very disappointing.

All of a sudden when you have to go, you have to go. Losing your grip. This is a simple bodily function, pal; don't try to inflate its importance.

Travels in the Land of Nod

*O*ne of the strange contradictions of middle age is that we are supposed to need less sleep but we get tired more easily.

I was driving up to the country one Friday evening a couple of winters ago when I noticed that I was more sensitive to the glare of headlights than ever before. After an hour or so on the road I also felt myself getting a bit drowsy. I turned up the radio. Some minutes later the drowsiness got worse. I even found myself blacking out for split seconds at a time. It was very scary. I changed the position of my seat—no good. I rolled down the window and a 25-degree wind blew through my car. The left side of my face was paralyzed with cold, my hair was whipping across my eyes, the radio was blaring with full quadriphonic fury and I was squeezed up against the steering wheel—knees against the dashboard—in a grotesquely unnatural and dangerous driving position.

I was now a horribly uncomfortable man falling asleep at the wheel. I slowed up a bit but the right front wheel would still occasionally drift onto the shoulder. I turned the overhead light on. For some reason I had thrown my head back and was looking down my nose as though I had half-glasses on. I knew of a gas station not far ahead that sold food and coffee, and was determined to make it there. What kept me going that night was the look of horror on the faces in the cars that passed me. As I made my way, shivering, to the coffee machine, there was a man just walking away with his coffee who looked at my wild hair, frozen half-face and drooping eyelids with a knowing glance. "The oddest thing happened," I tried to explain. "This never happened before. As I was driving . . ."

"Yeah, I know," he said, gulping down his coffee and staggering toward a convertible whose top was down.

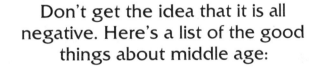

Don't get the idea that it is all negative. Here's a list of the good things about middle age:

1) It's not communicable.

Night Crawler

My eyes are open. It is dark. It is 3:20 A.M. I cannot see anything but the clock. My eyes have been this way for forty minutes and I believe this to be irrefutable evidence that I cannot sleep. I have thought it all through. I am not anxious, I do not feel bad, I am not overtired or undertired. The problem is clear: I cannot sleep.

I am not thinking about the kids or the office. But if you say you're not thinking about them you obviously are thinking about them or they wouldn't come to mind. When I get down to this line of reasoning, it's time to get up.

I dislike taking chemicals, so I go to the kitchen and warm up some milk (everyone says this works). I read while sipping hot milk—yuck—waiting for drowsiness. By 4:10 A.M. drowsiness still eludes me. It is now time to turn to chemicals. I go to the medicine cabinet and try, through a process of elimination and logic, to identify the sleeping pills among an array of prescription drugs all having wonderfully clinical-sounding names. I exclude everything that says it must be taken with meals or more than once a day and concentrate on bottles saying "when needed." Finally, I make my choice: It is either the right thing or it is the other possibility, which means spending the rest of the night in the bathroom. It is 4:25 and I'm starting to panic. I have to get up in two and a half hours. I take the risk and swallow the pill.

I stagger into the den and turn on the extremely late show and settle in, waiting for the pill to do its stuff.

It is 5:30 A.M. My eyes are open. I am watching yoga. I am not happy.

I've got it. I know what makes me sleepy—the Sunday *Times* crossword puzzle. I crawl over to the pile of newspapers in the corner and . . .

"Wake up, honey—it's seven o'clock. Why are you sleeping on *The New York Times?*"

As I stand at the sink washing the face of Hosni Mubarak from my forehead, where it had transferred itself from "The Week in Review," I wonder what my poor friends who complain of insomnia do and I am grateful I don't suffer from it.

Eubie Blake, who died a few years ago at the age of 100, said a week or so before his death, "If I'd known I was gonna live this long, I'd have taken better care of myself."

CHAPTER 3

EXERCISE AND THE MIDDLE-AGED MAN:
A Waist of Time

Test Stress

*C*urrent medical thinking strongly advocates the "stress test" for those of us in the "Masters" category or who are perceived to be middle-aged by our physicians. This is a test that measures the extent of damage other stresses of your life have left you with.

If you've never had one, it runs something like this: You show up one morning at an office that has an electronically controlled treadmill, a no-nonsense doctor and a nurse considerably stronger than yourself.

Don't eat much before trying this, and bring running shoes, shorts (you don't need a shirt) and a towel.

First you get a pep talk and are asked to sign a document acknowledging that you are aware this life-saving procedure could kill you and holding everyone in sight harmless.

Here's a helpful hint if you have hair on your chest: Do not schedule this procedure for late spring or summer, because the next thing that happens is that the nurse shaves your chest. Added to this humiliation is the fact that it's not your whole chest—just strips and patches here and there where the EKG leads are to be adhered to your flesh. The result is five or six weeks of looking like you've got mange. Walking around on the beach pointing to your chest saying "stress test" to explain what appears to be a terminal affliction produces no positive responses.

After all the leads are attached to your body, you are asked to breathe in and out very quickly (hyperventilate) to test all the dials, oscilloscopes and EKG stuff you're hooked up to. This is the point at which you start to really dislike the whole business. You look around the room and notice that it is filled with resuscitating equipment and portable cases with big red crosses on them. You have the decided feeling that there is an emergency about to occur and it could be you.

Now a few minutes of instruction, the main message of which is that this procedure doesn't work if you don't really go for it, really get stressed. On the treadmill, every three minutes the speed and the angle of incline are increased. You start at a fast walk and end up running for your life. Depending on your level of fitness, somewhere between 10 and 20 minutes after you start you are in a heavy sweat with a ganglion of wires slapping up against your body and your right arm being squeezed by the cuff of the sphygmomanometer (blood pressure measuring device). Your legs are getting really heavy and you're starting to get a bit lightheaded from oxygen deprivation. When your condition is just short of permanent brain damage, the doctor says something like "How are you doing? Can you go any further or would you like to stop now?" Invariably your answer is something wonderfully coherent like "Yaargggg . . . I . . . now . . . stop . . . you . . . dirty . . ." spoken hoarsely between gasps. At this point they crank the machine down rather quickly, hurl you onto a table and tell you not to move while everyone waits for your pulse to return to normal levels, which, you are sure, will take the better part of a week.

Within a half hour, however, you're on your way, albeit a bit wobbly. The results together with the evaluation of the administering doctor, are sent to your doctor and some days later he gives you his report. This could cause the ultimate in stress—except for the day you get the bill for all this, which has been known to produce stress of historic proportions.

My partner has been saying for years, "Why take a stress test if I am supposed to avoid stress?" None of my responses has ever moved him to take one. One of us is wrong.

Middle Age Lexicon

Words used exclusively (or more often) in middle age:

Prostate

Librium

What?

Ouch

Vitamin E

Escape

Cholesterol

Stress

Diet

Macho

Pritikin

Depression

*I*n any case, we all know that fitness and exercise are very important. Rust never sleeps. As we reach middle age, we become aware of certain negative forces at work, such as gravity and entropy, that don't even take a five-minute break in a lifetime.

In an obscure movie starring Carol Burnett and Elizabeth Taylor about middle-aged divorced and widowed women trying to get on with life, one says to the other: "Just as I get my head together my ass falls apart."

> Most middle-aged men who
> run away from home and family
> in order to find themselves
> go to California, because
> there's more light there.

The Picture of Boring and Gray

*T*he health words for today are diet and exercise. Easier said than done. Once you have stricken all carcinogens from your diet and reduced your intake to fodder, it's time to get your pulse rate down by regularly getting your pulse rate up. By a process of refinement, you decide to jog: no fancy equipment necessary; it can be done anywhere at any time.

One morning you get up early and decide this is it. Today is the first day of your physical comeback, a new way of life, healthy, svelte, desirable and macho. Well, you jump into your gear—running shoes, ankle socks, shorts, T-shirt with funny saying, black digital watch with beeper, and a sweat band (Heavy Hands and Walkman come later). Then you make the common and often paralyzing mistake of looking in the mirror.

EDWARDS

There in front of you is a poster for "before" that will never make it to "after." A gray, aging body with pale skinny legs sticking out of shorts straining to hold on to a midsection made of Twinkies. "I can't do this. I cannot run out into the streets of the city where I live and work and raise a family in children's clothing." At this point you start negotiating with yourself: "Maybe I should run earlier—when it's still dark out. How about tomorrow? Maybe the weekend." After a few minutes of that you end up compromising. You put on sunglasses and a cap and, ignoring the smirk on the doorman's face, slip out into the ranks of chugging and bobbing jocks running everywhere.

When Lecithin Is More

A friend recently went to his neighborhood health food store to get a fresh supply of iron ox-bile enzymes, granular Pacific sea kelp and pantothenic acid. (I think he was throwing a party.) While he was preparing to pay for these goodies, the checker-out looked at him and said, with a wink, "You know what you need? Zinc!" That's today's message, guys—zinc, heavy metal. For potency.

I don't believe in vitamins. I think you can get all the vitamins you need through proper diet. I do, however, take 1,000 mg's of vitamin C every morning just in case . . . and 100 mg's of E, which is supposed to be good for your memory, and . . . a multi, because I'm never sure about the minerals. Then there's . . .

To eat is human; to digest divine.
—Charles Townsend Copeland

Macrowave

*A*lthough we now know that eating is dangerous to one's health, we have, in middle age, a longing for Mom's cooking—to be a child again, I guess, or to feel the warmth of familiarity. Even if your mother's cooking was a violation of the Geneva Convention, it was what you knew and ate. Buddy Hackett used to say that all the years he was growing up at home he had terrible heartburn but didn't know what it was or that you weren't supposed to have it until he went into the army. In the army the heartburn stopped and he thought he was dying.

My mother, a daughter of the Russian Revolution, graduated from the school of "eating means health, and feeding means love." She loved feeding, I loved eating—a great combo. If it could have been arranged, we would have been at it around the clock. Chain eating. Compulsory education kept me from exploding at sixteen. With all the best intentions, she lovingly fed me the great ethnic diet of our cultural heritage, which today, when fed to Canadian rats, stops their hearts within 48 hours. A cholesterolarama. Our maple syrup was chicken fat. We could ingest enough oil in one meal to get A. J. Foyt 200 laps around Indianapolis. Not to mention salt, fat, sugar . . . who knew?

One middle-aged day I had a blood test. My blood looked like runoff from a McDonald's grill. The doctor became hysterical as it clogged his pipette; he told me if I didn't do something immediately, I would have to join OPEC. That turned things around: no fat, no salt, no sugar . . . ad nauseam. My mother still makes a

meal for me occasionally but can't figure out how to cook all the garbage I eat without using some sort of traditional lubricant.

The great mystery is that she's been eating the same artery-blocking swill for close to eighty years and appears unaffected by it. Maybe Mel Brooks is right about the indestructibility of little old Jewish ladies.

CHAPTER 4

MIDDLE AGE SEX: Where There's Smoke ...There's Smoke

> Middle age is the one time
> it's all right if you're not
> part of the solution
> because there isn't one.

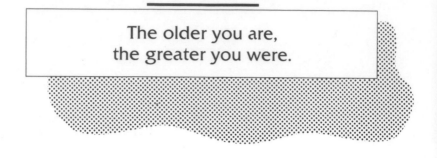

> The older you are,
> the greater you were.

Mammary
Deprivation

*L*oosely defined, mammary deprivation is the act of will that keeps us middle-aged men from staring at women's breasts if we feel we are being observed. The pressure of society. Here are obviously two of our favorite things and here we are pretending not to notice. Moreover, in most contexts they are clad or semi-clad or lifted or lit up in some way as to draw attention and we all play the game of nonchalance.

A very strange conflict. Only people of other cultures and construction workers are free from this problem.

Drool in the Sun

A sure sign of middle age is that, although we love seeing a "10" on the beach, we're willing to settle for two "5's." The May/December arrangement doesn't look so weird anymore and we view a lot of women as Pia Zadorable.

There is no question that we get less discriminating as the years go by. Compounding this condition is that in our lifetime we have seen women on the beaches go from conservative one-piece bathing suits to bikinis to topless—and on shore, braless and wearing pants so tight you would need the "jaws of life" to get them off. Meanwhile, men haven't changed a thing.

Some men make the case for older women on the grounds that they know more and therefore make better partners. But if knowledge of sexual behavior and responses is really so desirable, we would all be chasing Dr. Ruth.

It's all a question of perspective. When my daughter was quite young we bought her a kind of junior wallet that had, in the little plastic window on the inside, an identification card. On receiving the wallet, she immediately removed the card and filled it out. On the line next to the word Sex she wrote "No."

Erratic Zones

*T*his is a tough one: the psychodrama between you and your member. You and a partner are in an undescribed (not unimportant) circumstance and in a panic you realize that your gland has a mind of its own. It is thinking for itself or, worse, maybe it can't hear anymore. You take it into the next room and slap it around a little to reestablish your supremacy. No dice. Dead. Mr. Softy. Now you're really sweating. You make your exit mumbling something overly macho: "I must have been in free fall too long before pulling the cord this morning." "It could be my malaria again." And here comes the wacko part: You start talking to your organ. "What the hell is this? You were fine two days ago. I always thought we were in this together. Well, I was ready; where were you, you traitor?"

Very dangerous sign, talking to your member—worse if you start talking out loud.

The next day everything is working as usual but . . . it did happen. It is now forever a part of your mind and you will never really trust each other again. You're now living in the realm of carnal roulette, ever wary for the blank to come around. This dud's for you. But there's not much you can do about this since in reality (such a harsh word) it is your mind you cannot control. Remember the good old days when it was the other way around? Anyway you never lose your desire and you never stop trying, so it all averages out okay. If it gets bad, see a doctor. If it gets worse, see a nurse.

The Other America

We supposedly just had a sexual revolution. What side were you on? I'm still waiting at the Finland Station. Maybe we weren't meant to be participants in this one. I hardly knew about it until *Time* magazine ran a cover story about "Sex '80s Style" and explained that we had just come through a sexual revolution and it was now over. Apparently, I was not alone. Here are two letters to *Time* regarding the article:

I can tell you when the sexual revolution began: Oct. 29, 1969, at 4:20 P.M.—20 minutes after I got married!

Jim Greene
Whitestone, N.Y.

I am dismayed to learn that the revolution is over. Having missed it, I would be most grateful if you would announce a new one in the near future.

Bruce R. Vogel
San Mateo, Calif.

Well, if there really *was* a revolution, the incumbents are still in power.

Emission Controls

*A*fter the first couple of thousand orgasms in life, the whole business seems to lose some of the urgency associated with it in earlier years. You are no longer willing to risk life and limb for that moment of glory—consummation at any cost.

A doctor friend, with whom I jog occasionally, is convinced that God has given each of us just so many orgasms for our lifetime. One magazine, no reloading. He is preoccupied with the quandary of using them all up too early and being left without in his later years or not using them all up and dying with unspent, as it were, bullets. Personally I opt for the risk of running out. Maybe by the time I run dry, medical science will have perfected the private-parts transplant and one will need only to find some guy who has always thought sex to be dirty, dangerous and troublesome—all of which is true, but somebody's got to do it.

I must assume that the one-magazine theory includes self-abuse—after all, an orgasm is an orgasm. (Except in the case of women, where a lengthy debate has been going on about where it really occurs or is better or something. It's possible that *Cosmopolitan* has settled the question and I missed that issue.) Either way self-abuse is one of Homo sapiens's great glories. Forget higher intelligence, forget air-conditioning. It is man's only real advantage over other forms of life.

Eminence Sleaze

*S*elect the answer that most closely matches your own response.

When the possibility of an affair presents itself, your first thought is:
    A) Who has the energy for this?
    B) There's too much sexually transmitted stuff around.
    C) This could kill me.

When your wife has a headache, you suggest:
    A) two aspirins
    B) two hundred aspirins

If your wife goes on a trip without you and takes her diaphragm, you feel:
- A) She doesn't trust you.
- B) It's just habit.
- C) There's something you don't know.

If sexual contact with your wife is reduced to once a month or less, you are:
- A) unaware
- B) relieved
- C) exhausted

You are uneasy with phrases like:
- A) G spot
- B) Set me free.
- C) Hit my Go button.
- D) all of the above
- E) this entire book

When you wake up with an erection, you:
- A) Scream, "Not now, stupid!"
- B) Shake your head and go back to sleep.
- C) Reach for the Polaroid.

If your response to any of these situations is A, B, C, D or E, corrective or remedial measures will have no effect.

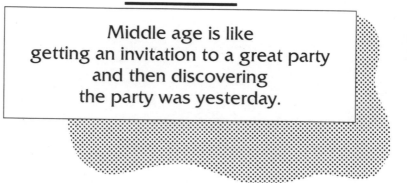

Middle age is like
getting an invitation to a great party
and then discovering
the party was yesterday.

Crash Landing

"**H**i, are you working this flight or are you just along for the ride?"

"I'm working. I'm just going to sit here through the take-off until we reach cruising altitude. Better buckle up now."

"Are you based in New York or L.A.?"

"L.A."

"I should have known by the tan. The climate is the only thing I like about L.A. I just go out for a couple of days at a time on business."

"Well, I think it's more a question of what you're doing and who you're doing it with. It could be anywhere if things are clicking for you, if you know what I mean."

"I'm sure you're right, but I only know business types in L.A."

"That must be awful. You've got to change that. I just know a few okay business types that I meet on the job. There are very few out where I live, though."

"Really. Where's that?"

"I share a place out at Malibu with three other girls. It's exhausting—party, party, party. But lots of fun. As a matter of fact, I hope this flight is on time because we're having a big open house party tonight. Lord knows who's going to show."

"Sounds great. But don't you, uh, have to worry about, you know, like weirdos showing up? I mean security and all that."

"Oh, that's so funny. You're just like my dad."

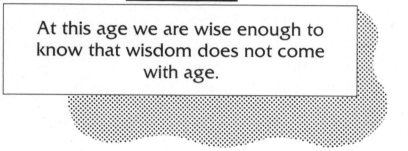

At this age we are wise enough to know that wisdom does not come with age.

CHAPTER 5

THE MIDDLE AGE PSYCHE

**MIDDLE AGE POPULATION DEMOGRAPHY
BY MENTAL STATE**

[WEIGHTED TO FACTOR OUT HYPOCHONDRIA
OF OTHER ORIGINS]

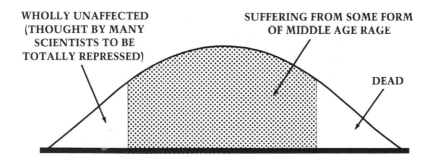

WHOLLY UNAFFECTED
(THOUGHT BY MANY
SCIENTISTS TO BE
TOTALLY REPRESSED)

SUFFERING FROM SOME FORM
OF MIDDLE AGE RAGE

DEAD

Errors of Omision

Usually when we say we don't remember some-thing it means that we cannot recall it. Certain things we really *do* forget—we have no recollection of them even when presented once again with the facts. But most often when we say we forgot to do something, it is a temporary condition and we soon remember what we forgot and therefore know we forgot it. "Shucks, I forgot to take my pill." "I forgot to pick up the paper." "I forgot to call so and so." Simple things, but annoying and sometimes scary.

To give you an illustration of this type of memory lapse, I am sure we have all by now played "Trivial Pursuit" with a group of our peers and watched each player, at one point or another, grimacing, struggling, saying "Hold it, I know that one. Hold on, just give me a minute . . . oh, God, I know it, wait . . ." We know, in this case, that we did not forget the information. It is a question of recall at will. The information will, no doubt, come back to us, though only when we don't need it.

A lot more serious is the second type of memory lapse, actually not remembering at all, ever, no matter what. Despite irrefutable evidence, you find yourself foolishly responding with phrases like: "I said that?" "That doesn't even *look* like my writing." Or, "You and I did what? Where? Who's Pookie?" Mystifying, to say the least.

The third type of memory lapse involves forgetting to remember and then remembering what you forgot. Since we cannot possibly remember everything all the

time, we weed out a lot of facts, images and sensory input all day long. The hard part is understanding how, after the deliberate procedures of driving somewhere, parking the car, locking the doors and walking to your destination, you can forget where you left two tons of automobile (sometimes with the keys locked inside . . . and the lights on).

There is a fourth type. But it escapes me for the moment.

Dialapse

You dial a telephone number and by the time someone answers, you have forgotten whom you are calling. This is a practical joke played on you by your mind, known as dialapse.

At first you feel weird but not yet embarrassed. Embarrassment occurs when you do not recognize the answering voice—no clue brings back the name of the callee or the purpose of the call. You are reduced to very few options. You can hang up, thereby avoiding risk but displaying cowardice. Or you can try and fake your way through it with a lie, saying something like "Is this the Public Library?" and hoping whoever it is will identify himself.

Sometimes I just wave a white flag and surrender, saying: "Hi! This is Fred Shoenberg and my mind has temporarily snapped. Could you please tell me who you are and why I am calling?"

People, for some reason, relate to that, and it softens the reaction.

Spontaneous, Spouse-Activated, Aural Dysfunction

*T*his is a recurring malady of middle age in which you cannot hear your wife. You are there. She is speaking and a built-in conditioned reflex directs you to say "Fine," or "That's okay," or "I'll take care of it." But you have no memory of her having spoken to you. So you go downtown and, of course, don't buy that last, very important item on the list. You don't know that your wife drove the station wagon through the back of the garage; you don't know that your son lost his $1,800 bite plate, and so on.

Later, when you learn about all these appalling calamities "again" for the first time, your wife says, "I told you that yesterday," or makes an even more mystifying accusation: "You never listen to a word I say." That you can hear.

Telepsy

*T*elepsy is a state brought about when the following conditions are in congruence: 1) the end of a long hard day at work; 2) availability of an armchair or couch; 3) the 6 o'clock news on TV. The symptoms here are: eyes closed, chin on chest, deep breathing and unintelligible sounds emanating from lips, which are frequently flapping.

To the lay person this condition often looks like sleep. The average duration is usually 15 minutes if not interrupted by a concerned relative. Family members should be educated about this disorder and cautioned about the dangers of breaking its continuity.

Brain Scam

*S*hould you find yourself doing something foolish or absentminded, you can save yourself considerable embarrassment by behaving as though you meant to do it that way, for reasons known only to you from the beginning. You will appear eccentric but not sclerotic.

You can learn this technique by observing cats. When a cat does something really klutzy, he pretends it is what he meant to do all along and just pauses, shakes himself and licks some part of his body for a while. I don't suggest the latter unless you are prepared to look outrageously eccentric.

Be aware that this technique does not work in every instance, for example, getting out of an airplane seat with your headset still plugged into your ears. Extreme example: A man steps up to a urinal, unbuttons his vest, takes out his tie and pees in his pants.

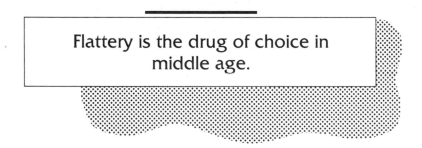

Flattery is the drug of choice in middle age.

The Dyspepsi Generation

I am sitting at home drinking beer and watching television. I am relaxed, even mellow—my guard is down. As it happens, an ad appears on the screen for the same beer I am drinking. It shows a group of very attractive people having a lot of fun in and around a body of water, while someone in the background is singing about how weekends were made for this beer. I am not upset, but I make a mental note about my age group not being represented among the revelers.

Next up is a commercial in which *only* my peers are in evidence. It's about Preparation H. "Wait a minute," I say to myself, suddenly feeling less mellow. I start paying more attention to the propaganda. Could this be yet another subliminal indignity to add to the growing list? I start keeping score.

My findings from that evening, in a nutshell, are that our gang only appears in ads using buzz words like:

regularity

hypertension

deficiency

insomnia

dentures

arthritis

indigestion

relief

and are absent in ads for:

> designer jeans
> chewing gum
> sports cars
> health clubs
> soft drinks
> skiing
> bathing suits
> anything sun-filled or sexually oriented.

Time Warps

"Are you mad? We just had the den redone a couple of years ago."

"That was 1968, dear."

"You are John's daughter? Aren't you supposed to be about twelve years old?"

"Next month is your brother's fiftieth birthday."

"Nonsense. How can he be fifty if I'm only . . . never mind."

Sudden Dearth

*F*urther to our discussion of memory lapses, I think it is worth pointing out that the problem can also occur in a business context.

Younger people with whom you are in business do not understand the phenomenon of middle-aged mind clog. They think it has to do with memory loss or sclerosis. Although the problem is very occasional (three or four times an hour) and benign (producing only mild hysteria), it can be disconcerting in a business setting.

I call this condition "Sudden Dearth" and have been experimenting with non-drug cures. The one action that appears to work on the symptom (nothing cures the syndrome) is called the Alzheimlich Maneuver, which works as follows: At the moment something you are trying to recall gets stuck in your mind, an alert associate or your secretary rushes up behind you, puts your head in an armlock, and squeezes until the irretrievable thought becomes dislodged.

The danger here is that you might first release a thought that got stuck the day before and went unliberated. You could be in the middle of a discussion on international trade and find yourself groping for Margaret Thatcher's name when someone applies the Alzheimlich Manuever and out comes "Roger Maris, sixty-one in 1961."

Most of the time, however, it works—if your business associates can live with slightly bizarre behavior.

CHAPTER 6

HEALTH

Down on the Pharm

*R*emember when we were really young and girls used euphemisms for everything "private," how it took all the courage we could muster to walk up to the counter at the local drug store and ask in a low voice for "a pack of Trojans, please." We expected all eyes to turn. They knew what sins we were about to commit, or thought we were going to commit—or hoped we would commit.

Today we blithely run down our list at the local drug store demanding Maalox, Head & Shoulders, a refill of a Valium prescription, Visine, a diuretic, sleeping pills, extra strength Tylenol, appetite suppressants, hypertension pills, industrial strength mouthwash, a couple of Dr. Scholl's inserts . . .

My pharmacist is obvious in his concern that I keep my account current. From observing my weekly orders, he knows it can't be long now.

> By now you must realize that middle age, if not treated properly, could kill you.

The Plot Sickens

*H*ypochondria, although a bit screwy, has its rewards. Despite your constantly contracting new ailments, you discover, after all, that you are cured of whatever you thought you had last week.

Well, you wake up one morning and there's a spot on your face, or the back of your hand, that you never saw before and you're sure it's cancer. Your eyesight has been getting steadily worse: brain tumor. A little gas: heart attack. Pretty soon you're showing symptoms of whatever ailment you saw on television the night before. I call it "disease du jour."

Exacerbating all this is the as yet undiagnosed major aggravant—middle age rage.

A ray of hope: It is statistically impossible to have a different form of cancer every morning.

Many years ago, my dear friend Harvey and I, together with a small group of people, spent a long weekend in Connecticut at the house of another friend. On the second morning, I noticed Harvey was somewhat subdued and did not go for a swim in the lake, as was his custom. Also, he had cotton sticking out of his right ear. Not wanting to confront him directly, I asked his wife what the problem was. "Harvey woke up this morning and couldn't hear with his right ear and is hoping that it has something to do with too much swimming yesterday—water in the ear or some such thing, but actually he's convinced it's a brain tumor." "Does that sort of thing happen so suddenly?" I asked. "With him it does," she replied. Harvey is a dozen or so years older than I am and was in early middle age at the time.

None of us took this too seriously, and as one of our party would appear at lakeside and ask, "What's with Harvey?" another would say, "Oh, it's a brain tumor. He's not swimming today." This nonchalance wasn't doing much for Harvey. The next day his hearing was worse and he was getting a little panicky. Fortunately, it was now Sunday and we would be heading for New York, where he would see a specialist Monday morning.

Monday at noon I got the news. At some enormous expense Harvey had put himself in the hands of the foremost "ear man" in New York, who, after removing the cotton from Harvey's ear and looking farther down in the ear canal, found more cotton. A loose Q-Tip had lodged in his ear and was, needless to say, impairing his hearing. Harvey was cured.

The only thing the doctor said was, "Well, I guess you're not going to do that again."

That was the year we created the annual award for the most extraordinary false diagnosis. Over the years we have found that each of us has had at least one that qualified. In any case, that year, Harvey narrowly beat out another friend who insisted that, despite a 30-pound weight gain, his collar size was still the same as when he was in college. One night he was convinced he had spontaneous asphyxia and wrote a holographic will naming me executor.

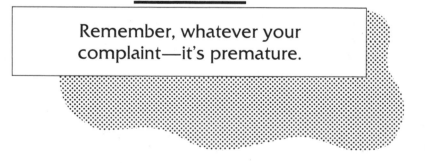

Remember, whatever your complaint—it's premature.

Present Tense

Stress is the exercise of the mind's right to behave irrationally in its pursuit of depression.

Stress is not hereditary but it will find your weakness and work on it until it gives you something that is. This doesn't mean you won't die from something personal and wonderful that is all your own; after all, individuality and self-respect must still be considered. There is also a question of susceptibility. I was convinced I had contracted an obscure Oriental disorder when my doctor told me I had "Taipei" behavior. "Type A" notwithstanding, if you are really good at it, you can get stress from almost anything—radical surgery, cream cheese or a nap.

The avoidance of stress is a major preoccupation and a minor industry today. Stress management for a lot of people comes in pill, liquid or powdered form—from Coke to coke in one generation. Needless to say, this is the wrong approach.

Most stress can be alleviated by simply not thinking about your job, money, sex, mortality or the Mets. The remainder is little stuff that can be easily controlled by winning the lottery, eating a pint of ice cream or by Raquel Welch with a cattle prod.

Major Stress-Inducing Phrases

1. "Hi, Grandpa."

2. "Can I carry that for you?"

3. "I'm sure you and your daughter will like this room."

4. "May I show you something more, uh, conservative?"

5. "I'm sorry, sir, but according to this tape measure you're a size larger than that."

6. "Keep running . . . go for it . . . you can make it, Pop."

7. "You're probably looking for bonds with a shorter maturity."

8. "Sorry, sir. This prescription has been filled twenty-seven times and was originally issued for a temporary disorder."

The Theory of
Relativity

*M*ost of what we have been examining or com-
plaining about thus far has been influenced
by our genes—hair, eyes, body types and certain weaknesses. As we will, in the not too distant future, find
ourselves in a life-and-death struggle with our genes,
it is therefore worth a look at where we are coming
from. Look at your parents and grandparents, their ailments, weaknesses and tendencies, and what they died
from. Obviously not everything is hereditary; we do a
lot of damage on our own. If you're not sure of the
cause of what's ailing you—heredity or environment
—give the nod to the environment. It's a bit late for
the other.

In researching your family chart to determine
where the genetic weaknesses are, remember that
everyone has to die of something; you don't just die of
old age. If Aunt Rose, for example, was hit by a bus, it
doesn't mean much. If, however, another relative, at
another time and place, was also killed by a bus, I
would be a bit concerned. The reason for going through
this exercise is obviously to be able to hold off the
inevitable for a while. Forewarned, and so forth. It
seems that, to some degree, those who remember the
past are also condemned to repeat it.

The following chart will give you some idea of how to reconstruct your lineal departures:

HYPOTHETICAL GENEALOGY
Tracing Causes of Death

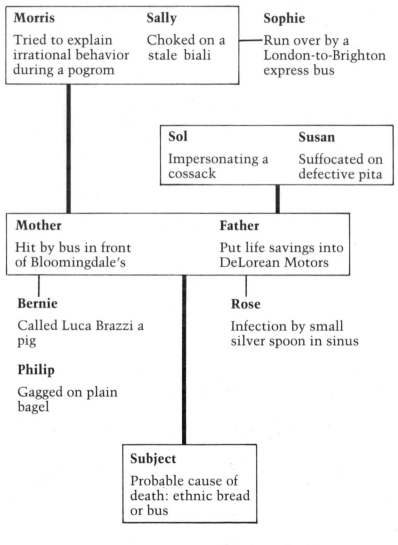

Morris

Tried to explain irrational behavior during a pogrom

Sally

Choked on a stale biali

Sophie

Run over by a London-to-Brighton express bus

Sol

Impersonating a cossack

Susan

Suffocated on defective pita

Mother

Hit by bus in front of Bloomingdale's

Father

Put life savings into DeLorean Motors

Bernie

Called Luca Brazzi a pig

Rose

Infection by small silver spoon in sinus

Philip

Gagged on plain bagel

Subject

Probable cause of death: ethnic bread or bus

. . . You get the idea.

CHAPTER 7

LIFE-STYLES OF THE MIDDLE-AGED MAN

Placido Domingo

Sunday is the essential health preserver and stress controller for middle-aged man. Wives, children and other family members must understand how critical his total self-indulgence on Sunday is. It is his right. It is so written. The Sabbath. Pro football, large newspapers, crossword puzzles, perhaps even beer, bring him closer to God and restore his health.

In the off-season, when it may appear that he has more time, certain things should not even be discussed on Sundays:

Mothers

Mothers-in-law

Lawns

Shaving

Children

Church

Exercise

If observed, these procedures could bring him within a football's length of the true meaning of peace. Such a small thing to ask.

Huh?

---

*P*acing oneself becomes increasingly important as the years go by.

Some things cannot be effectively accelerated. It's a waste of effort and energy to run out of your apartment building screaming at the doorman, "I'm in a terrible hurry. Get me two taxis."

Afterthoughts

*T*here are two major divergent attitudes about death (and life). One goes: "Life sucks and then you die"—a minimalist's negative approach. Here's the one I like: "Only suckers die."

Although none of us has the slightest intention of dying when we arrive at middle age, it is hard to escape the notion altogether. There are lots of reminders about. The most troublesome for me are the friendly insurance folks who tell us that dying without proper coverage is the grossest form of negligence and cruelty and demonstrates a stupid and loathsome disregard for one's family. Wow! Wait, don't label me with that—I'll buy.

You also have the responsibility of choosing the "right" policy. The insurance industry has more products than 3M. The one I like most is "Whole Life" because it suggests that all the others are partial or fragments.

There are some insurance pitches that make you feel great: "I can get you covered for $100,000 without a physical." The clear implication is that, in his opinion, you haven't a prayer of passing one. Or "Let's face it, guys like you—Type A, workaholics—you could go like that (finger snap) and you're not prepared. Someone as smart in business as you are, it's criminal."

You start getting mail about buying a little piece of real estate as your final resting place—the ultimate condo.

Some of us, no doubt, are having more trouble staying alive than others, but there are a few who are out of control. Do you go beyond a modest contemplation of your mortality when encountering phrases such as: "Do not use after April 20, 1988," "This lane ends 100 feet," or "The flight you're on terminates in New York." If so, and you have gone through the middle age rage zone and over the edge, you're likely to be in Venice, California, on a skateboard next week.

... There's a Way

*T*he Will: a monument to "What If." After days of discussion with your lawyer, you are reduced to contemplating things like "What if you and your wife, together with the children, your mother, the cat, both grandchildren, and an eccentric aunt all perished in some ghastly disaster but your wife died five minutes before you, your first wife is not remarried and your executor is on the SEC's hit list?" If you really want to do right by everybody, you can spring for 50 or 60 pages of trusts, the end result of which would be that no one pays any taxes anywhere and everyone gets a lot of money but they can't spend it and all the objets d'art are left to a museum in Istanbul, which gets delivery when the last person in your line carrying your name perishes of natural causes.

After spending a significant portion of your estate for this document, you begin imagining yourself years hence being wheeled around the boardwalk, unable to do anything but gurgle and long for a return to the condition you were in when they only called you gaga, when someone tells you about the Tax Reform Act of 2023, which has just turned your will into a roll of Charmin.

Off the Wrack

I got a strong message one day that I should own a Giorgio Armani suit, the draped, tapered, one-button double-breasted look that says "chic" and "now" loud and clear. I couldn't wait. This was going to be my clothing statement for the winter season—smart, youthful, stylish. The fact that I was somewhat overweight and that my body tapered in the wrong direction did not deter me.

I drove down to Barney's and made my way to the Giorgio Armani Room (an entire room devoted to my future wardrobe). As I stood in the doorway, taking a deep breath, trying to calm my excitement, the salesman, a small, thin, overdressed young man of questionable orientation (really not much question) looked me over, closed his eyes and shook his head in an emphatically negative manner. I was stunned. Surely he didn't mean me. I looked around quickly. There was no one else in the Giorgio Armani room. I pointed to myself and arched my eyebrows into plaintive question marks as if to say, "Surely you don't mean that you don't have a suit to fit this hulk?" Once again, the same response, the lowered eyes, the shaking head. Rejected, crushed, returned to the world of non-designer suits in total silence, and not a word exchanged. I thought for a moment about doing something terrible and violent to this destroyer of dreams and images and would have had I not been sure he would have enjoyed it. I got into my car and headed back uptown thinking about maybe getting a tattoo.

You have, no doubt, been exposed to numerous hazards in life that promised great physical and mental discomfort. Middle age delivers.

Atmospherically Generated Fabric Contraction

Wherein your summer suits, which have been hanging in the back of a closet for eight months, no longer fit in the spring.

Do not blame the suits!

Resist, also, a strong tendency to blame the dry cleaner.

The probable cause is bagel retention.

Second-Hand Rows

I went to a thrift shop ("antique clothing empor-
ium") with my daughter so she could buy a new
used coat for winter. It is very in to wear something
that far out. While she was trying on old moth-eaten
rags, I sauntered over to the men's area. There, hanging
in neat rows, was my entire wardrobe from the fifties
including ties and band jacket. Can't they wait until
we are gone? Must we suffer the humiliation of seeing
armies of children running around in outsized, recon-
stituted clothing from another age—our youth? My
sports jacket, which was once groovy, is now funky.
Never mind that it seems as if I just took those clothes
to the dry cleaner's yesterday, they all look awful. It's
as though we'd had a mass dementia then.

Hint: Do not save your Mao jacket any longer. It's
not coming back. Even if it does, you don't want it.

As we stood waiting to pay for the remnants my
daughter had picked out, I overheard one of two gig-
gling girls holding a replica of one of my old sports
jackets in front of a mirror saying: "Can you imagine
some nerd buying this because he actually liked it—I
mean straight, I mean not funk? I wonder if he's still
alive somewhere."

Flycheck

A conditioned reflex developed by modern western culture: checking to make sure our flies are zippered in the up, or closed, position. As we get older, we either start to lose faith in the quality of the new generation of zippers and fear that they will, of their own capriciousness, open spontaneously, or think we may have forgotten to zip them up.

I have caught myself in mid flycheck with an overcoat and double-breasted suit on. It wouldn't have mattered had I no pants on at all, and there I was checking the old zipper.

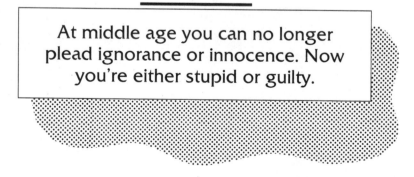

At middle age you can no longer plead ignorance or innocence. Now you're either stupid or guilty.

Going Through Customs

*W*e were brought up to believe, and rightly so, that one cannot change the rules in the middle of the game. It's not *fair!*

Much to my dismay—something of which we have substantially greater amounts in middle age—that's exactly what's been happening during our lifetimes. Slowly, without our immediate perception, they have buried Hoyle and banished the Marquis of Queensberry and have rewritten or disregarded lots of stuff.

For example, when we were kids, who smoked? Everybody smoked. Roosevelt smoked, Churchill smoked, Babe Ruth smoked, John Wayne smoked, everybody in all the movies smoked (Paul Henreid even lit up two at a time and gave one to Bette Davis). It was cool, it was sophisticated, it was what you did. Well, if you're still doing it you're a pariah, a weak-willed, spineless and selfish person with little or no character. You went from regular guy to outcast without changing a thing. How do you make that sort of transition without suffering real psychological damage? You don't. We were passive, minding our own business, as the world's finger of health, decency and righteousness slowly turned and pointed straight at us. Hey, what about our heroes? As we look around for help we realize they're all gone. You're on your own, pal. It's enough to turn one to drink.

Guess who drank? Everybody drank. Social drinks,

ethnic drinks; weddings, wakes; hooch, swill, booze, grog, firewater . . .

Care to take a shot at what's in disfavor now?

Guess who ate steaks, hamburgers, sausage, salt, sugar? Very confusing stuff.

You bought a little plot on the edge of town and built your dream house and twenty years later you find out they were dumping something weird there during the war and now your kids light up in the dark.

I don't think this is nostalgia. This is a problem of long-term, hand-me-down, subliminal thought screw-up. Twenty-five years on the Disorient Express. Now black is white and everything is upside-down and we're supposed to cope, to adjust. This is not nostalgia —this is neuralgia.

There used to be some mystery and a little confusion about sex and certain social mores and such. But now, between Donahue and *Cosmopolitan*, we know it all. We know more than all. We know more than is.

There used to be a dress code, nothing fancy or serious, but it was okay, no one had to guess anything, it was right out there, it was up front. Today young guys come to the office looking like Boy Madonna, and you spend a lot of time wondering What? Why?

Wasn't asbestos a lifesaver?

Weren't the Japanese the bad guys?

What the hell is going on?

Who can learn all the new rules?

Who wants to?

Let's just hold on to the good old values for a little while longer.

CHAPTER 8

FUTURE SCHLOCK

Middle age is when
you suddenly find that
your parents are old,
your kids are grown up,
and you haven't changed.

Youthanasia

*F*or example, you feel an almost uncontrollable desire to smite your child who, during a serious dinner party at your home, appears straight from college looking like a yeti in running clothes. He offers the first person he engages in conversation a controlled substance, and tells him that his values suck.

The Son Also Rises

A friend in the textile trade decided to take a real vacation after thirty years of building his business. A three-month cruise around the world. A confirmed Type A, he had already had some sort of heart episode; it was time to get away. The reason he was able to do this without worry was that, much to his great fortune, he had a genius for a son who was going to look after things in his absence. A son who had graduated with honors from college and business school and who, quite remarkably, knew everything. What luck.

After a hundred days my friend returned to the office totally rested and beautifully tanned.

"Welcome back, Dad."

"Hello there, Son. How did things go?"

"Great."

"Why is there a television set on my desk? I don't like television. I only watch the news."

"It's not a TV. It's a computer."

"Okay. Why is there a computer on my desk? I don't like games either."

"It's not for games; it's for running the business."

"How can it run the business? *I* run the business."

"I mean it helps run the business more efficiently."

"For example."

"It keeps all the receivables, payables, inventory and billing up to the minute."

"Benny the bookkeeper and I have been doing the inventory for thirty years without problems."

"I retired Benny the bookkeeper."

"What the hell do you mean, retired? How could you get rid of Benny the bookkeeper? He's been with me from the beginning."

"He was getting too old for the job and he was doing a lot of strange things. I found him . . . Dad, I'm trying to explain something to you and you're putting little white pills under your tongue. Please try to pay attention. I found him keeping certain records and inventories in pencil. Now you know no one would do that unless he felt he might have to change them later for some reason."

"A genius."

"Now everything is in the computer and gets recorded automatically and a printout goes straight to our auditors. But that's just the beginning. Wait till you hear what else it does. I've already cut sixty percent of our employees."

"What do you mean *our?*"

"Well, uh, I work here too, don't I?"

"Not any more."

"What do you mean?"

"You're fired."

"You can't fire me. I'm your son."

"I can and you're not."

Just When You Thought It Was Safe to Go Back on the Dance Floor

*C*hildren spinning on their faces, whirling on their backs, flailing their limbs and dancing with short spasmodic movements as though performing on a third rail. A great contribution to our culture. Maybe that's unfair. We jitterbugged and twisted and I don't remember my parents doing either. We were brought up primarily with "social dancing." It required a partner. He led, she followed. Also, it called for touching. Basically a joint effort. I think that's my main objection. Not only can we no longer distinguish between the sexes among our young but with break-dancing it's a solo performance. If you try to do it *with* someone, it not only takes on the appearance of some martial arts maneuver, it's physically dangerous.

If you were brought up, as I was, sort of middle class (although I'm sure my father would have upgraded us to business class had it been available at the time), you learned prehistoric steps such as the rhumba, samba, fox-trot and lindy. We don't hear that sort of music any more. But, then, we don't dance that much any more either.

We were all in at the beginning of rock and watched and listened to its evolution. If you haven't been to a disco for a while, let me assure you that it is still a worthwhile experience with only three minor side effects:

1) While there, you may feel like a chaperone.

2) The next morning your physical sensations are indistinguishable from what you feel the morning after a stress test.

3) For the following twenty-four hours there is an intermittent ringing in your ears, which may cause you to pick up the telephone several times unnecessarily.

A teenager when requested to perform a household chore travels at the speed of dark.

Who's Sari Now?

We must also thank today's youth for adding to our lexicon such words as ashram, mantra, nirvana and tandoori—not to mention giving us a greater understanding of eastern cultures.

Some years ago our son started following a guru and moved into an ashram in New York. The guru has since died and has been replaced by two gurus (gurim? guri?). Well, at first I was convinced that this was just another normal tasteless rebellion against the establishment, our values, western culture, the bomb, meat, money, work and shoes. But as a modern, wonderfully understanding parent, I did not want to confront him with these suspicions without first learning more about what he was doing. I set about reading some of the literature, lunched at the ashram a few times and listened to some other followers. Then my lucky day came. I was invited to attend an "intensive." This is the part that's hard at middle age. I found myself in a dark room with a hundred other people sitting on the floor (on a rug), without shoes, cross-legged in the yoga position, for three and a half hours. Most of the time we chanted and repeated a mantra. After about the first hour of this my son leaned over and whispered, "Do you feel anything yet?" "Yes," I replied, "my back is killing me."

We still had several hours of being twisted up in this position to go. I must confess, however, that the crippling pain in my lower back dimmed rapidly when I realized I could no longer walk.

It has been difficult for my wife and me to assimilate all the wonderful teachings we have been presented with—especially the opportunity to call our son by a name unknown this side of Jaipur. Such is our karma.

Overheard in the Hallways

"How about lunch? I could use a martini or two right about now."

"Thanks, but I have a date to play squash and then I thought I'd run a fast three miles and grab a salad and some carrot juice on the way back to the office."

"Sure, no problem. I did that yesterday. Maybe one day next week."

"Hi, how was the long weekend?"

"Well, I flew down to Club Med in Cancún and blew all my beads on a blond word processor with a turbo-charged body and a thirst for life. How about you?"

"Well, Muriel and I drove down to see one of the kids at school and took in a show—I mean, it was just great."

CHAPTER 9

TRAVAIL BUREAU

**Middle-aged man's retrospective view
(in graphic form) of why
he did not attain greater success.**

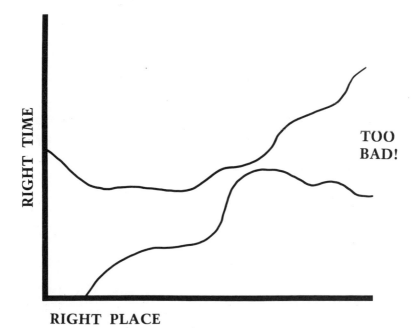

Executive Search

You are most likely a middle-aged businessman if:

1) You yearn for a return to the days when secretaries made coffee and served it.

2) You were not asked to join the softball team this year.

3) You think "yuppie" is something Tom Mix used to say.

4) You discover that the management person who never quite understood and was resistant to change and new ideas is now you.

5) You find yourself hiring people who are peers of your children, and wondering what their rooms look like.

6) You are DWI after one Cuba Libre at lunch with the boys.

7) A few beers at the ball game, and you sense imminent incontinence.

8) Young people in your office looking at some article of your clothing say something like, "It will probably come back."

CHAPTER 10

NOW THAT WE'RE HERE

A Revolting Development

*A*dulthood is something few of us are ready for, suited to, or comfortable with. Somewhere in the scheme of things a sort of retardation sets in. Our fathers seemed to be up to it. Lord knows our grandfathers were certainly adults.

It is something we didn't ask for or want and therefore don't exemplify terribly well. Most of us are involved in a Peter Principle scenario in which we have been automatically elevated to a level of incompetence. Maturity, up to a point, was once enough. But this business about responsibility, judgment, family, community, mankind. You can't mean me. I just hung up my skates. I'm still working on Me.

No place to hide, fellows. Between adolescence and middle age—the DMZ—you can fake it, being neither here nor there. But now, this is it—hard ball. We actually have to function as grown-ups. Boy, if they only knew. It's 10:00 P.M. Do you know where your childishness is? Yes; suppressed.

Well, we're all out here winging it and trying to look serious and wondering how it all happened. On a day filled with such wondering recently I received some correspondence concerning my 30th high school reunion. Along with the letter discussing possible alternatives was a book listing all members of the graduating class who could be located, their addresses and their professions. As I glanced through the list, I was amazed to find how many of my peers had made it to adulthood, some even in a "serious" way.

There was a fellow on the list who 32 years ago would call up the school and say in a high squeaky voice, "Myron can't come to school today. He has a terrible cold. This is my mother speaking." And now he's a judge. There was another guy on the list who once inadvertently nailed his jacket into the shop project we were working on. Then, when he discovered his mistake, he sawed off the bottom of his jacket rather than disturb the project. He's now a famous surgeon. And then there were all those nerds and weirdos and freaky girls and dorks and they're all adults now, too, and it's so frightening I'm not sure I can go to this reunion thing.

We're all up here now and running the world—no wonder we're so worried.

> *When I was young I thought that people at the top really understood what the hell was happening . . . whether they were cardinals or bishops or generals or politicians or business leaders. They knew. Well, I'm up there, and now I know they don't know.*
>
> *—David Mahoney (ex-chairman and CEO of Norton Simon, Inc.)*

Try to remember that, with the exception of your parents and your children, most people will consider you an adult.

Rules to Live By in Middle Age:

1) Never use catchy philosophical phrases like: "The best is yet to come" or "We are about to enter the golden years."

2) Be realistic. Avoid delusions of adequacy.

3) Have a sexual experience at least twice a week, even if it has to be with something inanimate (don't ask), until further notice. .

4) Remember, wealth and power are still more attractive than youth. So . . .

5) Do not try to look 25. You won't.

6) Don't slow up on purpose. Nature has its own braking system.

7) There's no remission from middle age. (Just in case you're waiting for it.)

8) Middle age is mostly side effects and behavioral deviations—the heavy stuff is still out there.

A Couple of
Suggestions for
Fighting Back

Get up, in a public conveyance, and offer your seat to someone your age or slightly younger.

Utilize *Sportspeak*. Examples: When someone calls early Sunday morning, answer the telephone breathlessly, gasping for air, and say "Hang on a second, I just want to take off my running shoes." Pause. "Did you call earlier? I've been out for quite a while." Or "Hold on, I just have to put these weights away."

And stuff like that . . .

LAST CHAPTER

HOW TO AVOID MIDDLE AGE

Wait a minute, it's coming to me . . .

ACKNOWLEDGMENTS

A grateful acknowledgment to Marilyn Wells, Rick Bell, Kristen Bratberg and Michael Rosen (none of whom is middle-aged), who helped me in areas where I have a total lack of skills: word- and thought-processing.

ABOUT THE AUTHOR

Fred Shoenberg has been working on this book for forty-nine years. He was born in Rumania (which was too much like the Middle Ages) and grew up on the Upper West Side of New York—living with his parents until they reached middle age. After a brief appearance at Syracuse University he went to Wall Street, where sixteen years ago he and his partner (of the same age) started the investment firm of Shoenberg Hieber, Inc.

Mr. Shoenberg now lives on the East Side of Manhattan (where there are more middle-aged people) and spends his weekends on a farm in Dutchess County, where he appears ageless. Coinciding with the publication of this book is Mr. Shoenberg's fiftieth birthday; he is survived by his wife and two children.